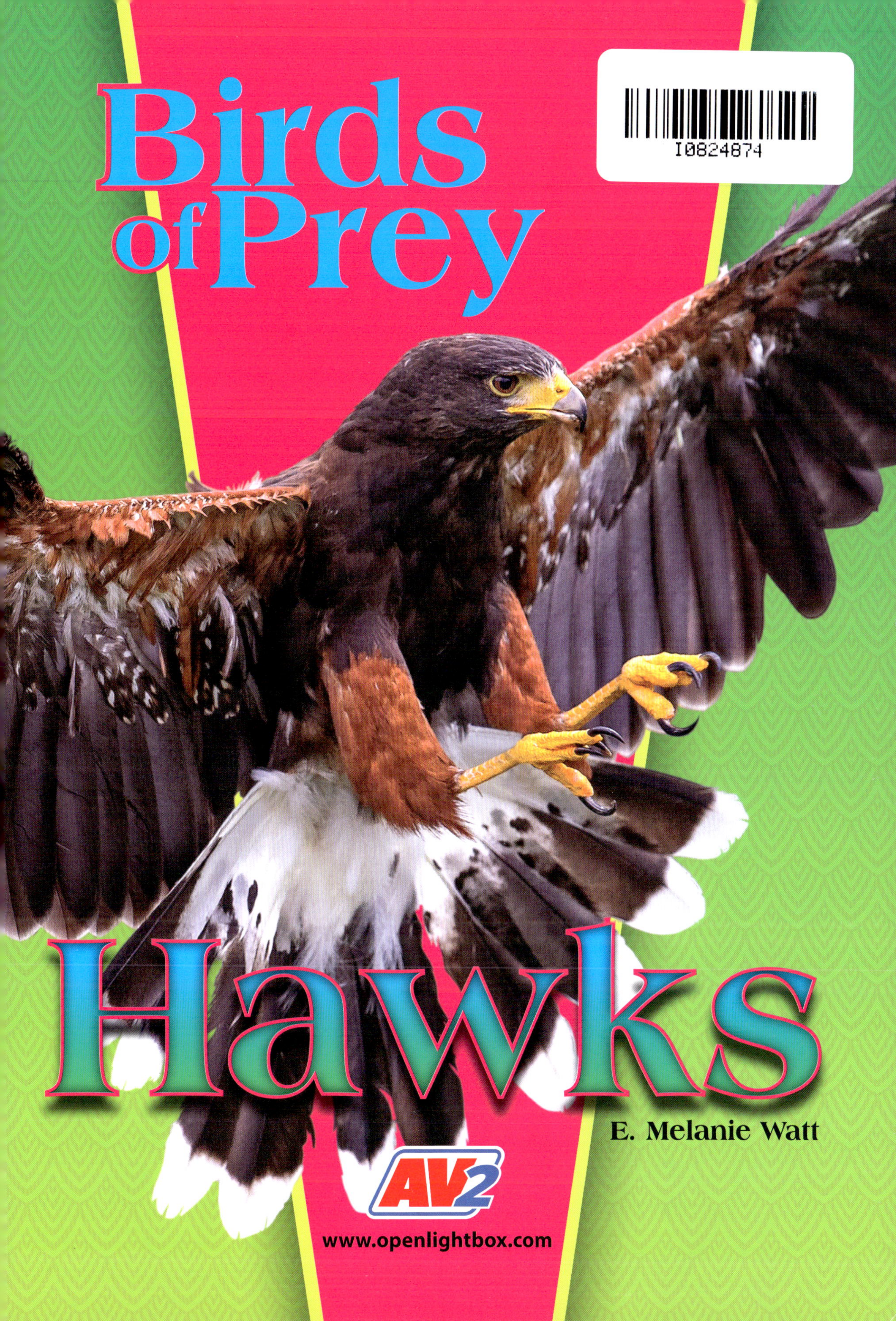

Birds of Prey

Hawks

E. Melanie Watt

AV2

www.openlightbox.com

Step 1
Go to **www.openlightbox.com**

Step 2
Enter this unique code
WUNQHG32O

Step 3
Explore your interactive eBook!

AV2 is optimized for use on any device

Your interactive eBook comes with...

Contents
Browse a live contents page to easily navigate through resources

Audio
Listen to sections of the book read aloud

Videos
Watch informative video clips

Weblinks
Gain additional information for research

Slideshows
View images and captions

Try This!
Complete activities and hands-on experiments

Key Words
Study vocabulary, and complete a matching word activity

Quizzes
Test your knowledge

Share
Share titles within your Learning Management System (LMS) or Library Circulation System

Citation
Create bibliographical references following the Chicago Manual of Style

This title is part of our AV2 digital subscription

1-Year K–5 Subscription
ISBN 978-1-7911-3320-7

Access hundreds of AV2 titles with our digital subscription.
Sign up for a FREE trial at **www.openlightbox.com/trial**

Hawks

CONTENTS

Meet the Hawk

Hawks belong to a group of birds known as raptors, or birds of **prey**. Raptors also include eagles, falcons, and owls. Hawks, eagles, and falcons are diurnal, meaning they hunt and are active during the day and sleep at night. Owls are often nocturnal, meaning they are active at night.

The word "hawk" is often used to describe medium-sized raptors that share certain traits. These birds have wings that are wide, rounded, and spread out like fingers at the tips. Hawks have hooked beaks and use their strong, sharp, curved **talons** to grasp their prey.

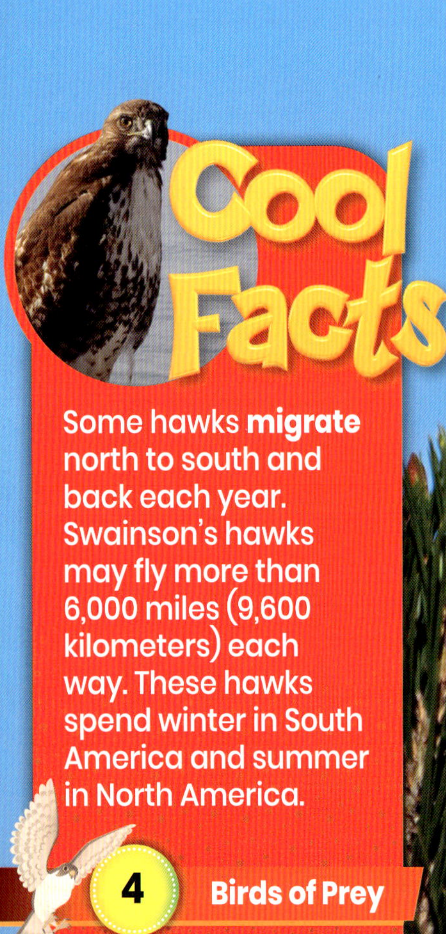

Some hawks **migrate** north to south and back each year. Swainson's hawks may fly more than 6,000 miles (9,600 kilometers) each way. These hawks spend winter in South America and summer in North America.

Types of Hawks

Although all hawk **species** share common features, they have a wide range of different shapes, colors, and sizes.

Bicolored Hawk
(*Accipiter bicolor*)

Ferruginous Hawk
(*Buteo regalis*)

Madagascar Sparrowhawk
(*Accipiter madagascariensis*)

Northern Goshawk
(*Accipiter gentilis*)

Slate-Colored Hawk
(*Buteogallus schistaceus*)

Swainson's Hawk
(*Buteo swainsoni*)

Tiny Hawk
(*Accipiter superciliosus*)

White-Necked Hawk
(*Buteogallus lacernulatus*)

Hawk Features

Hawks have many **adaptations** that help them hunt. One of their most important senses is sight. A hawk's vision helps it hunt during the day.

Cool Facts

When an osprey, also known as a sea hawk, dives into water to catch fish, it closes a third eyelid. This protects the bird's eyes while still allowing it to see underwater.

WINGS
The wing size and shape of a hawk species depends on its **habitat** and hunting style. Many have broad wings that allow them to soar for long periods without flapping.

EARS
Hawks have an excellent sense of hearing, which helps them to locate prey.
BEAK
Sharp, hooked beaks help hawks bite and tear food.
TALONS
Hawks use their talons to catch, kill, and carry prey, along with building and defending their nests.
EYES
Hawks are known for their eyesight. A red-tailed hawk can see mouse-sized prey 100 feet (30 meters) away.

Size and Shape

Most hawks are in the buteo or accipiter groups of raptors. Buteo hawks are often called soaring, or grassland, hawks. They are large, with long, wide, rounded wings and short tails. Accipiter hawks are often called forest hawks. These hawks tend to have shorter, rounded wings and longer, rudder-like tails that allow them to maneuver between trees.

Ospreys make up their own group. They are large birds with slim bodies, and long, narrow wings. Their wings make an "m" shape when they fly.

Female and male hawks often look quite similar. However, females are usually larger than males. In some cases, they can be twice as big as male hawks.

The diet of a sharp-shinned hawk is made up almost entirely of smaller birds. Males of this species are the smallest hawks in North America.

Hawk Wingspans

Little Sparrowhawk
Wingspan
Between 15 and 21 inches (38 and 53 centimeters)

Sharp-Shinned Hawk
Wingspan
Between 21 and 26 inches (53 and 66 cm)

Cooper's Hawk
Wingspan
Between 27 and 37 inches (69 and 94 cm)

Red-Tailed Hawk
Wingspan
Between 38 and 56 inches (97 and 142 cm)

Ferruginous Hawk
Wingspan
Between 52 and 56 inches (132 and 142 cm)

Osprey
Wingspan
Between 59 and 71 inches (150 and 180 cm)

Hawk Habitats

Hawks live in many different habitats around the world, except for those in the extreme polar regions. Within these homes, hawks need to hunt for prey, find mates, build nests, and raise their young. Many species migrate between habitats. Hawks live both in **tropical** places, with high rainfall, and in dry areas, with little to no rain. They also live in places that change between being warm and cold with the season.

Hawk habitats include forests, meadows, grasslands, deserts, rainforests, marshes, wetlands, and many more. Some species of hawks can also be found on farmland, in parks, and in large cities. Hawks often build their nests in trees or on cliff ledges. Some live high up on utility poles, on buildings, or even on window ledges.

Red-tailed hawks are highly adaptable. They can be found as far north as Alaska and as far south as Venezuela, in South America.

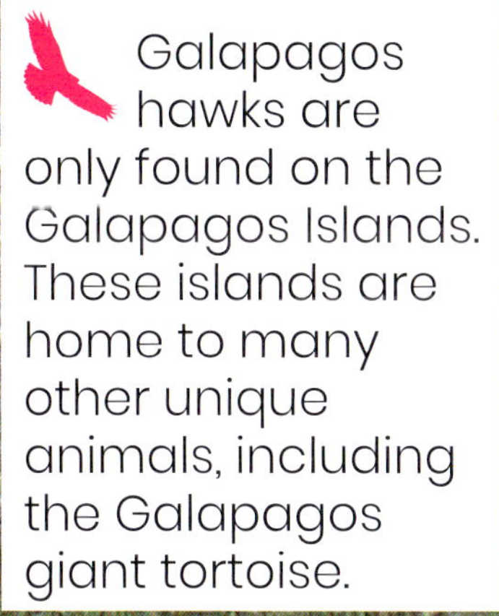

Galapagos hawks are only found on the Galapagos Islands. These islands are home to many other unique animals, including the Galapagos giant tortoise.

Hawks save energy by soaring, swirling in the air using warm air currents. The birds look like objects being stirred in a pot or kettle. This is why a group of hawks in the sky is called a kettle.

Life Cycle

Hawks use many different displays, sounds, and other behaviors to attract mates. Pairs of hawks often stay together for life.

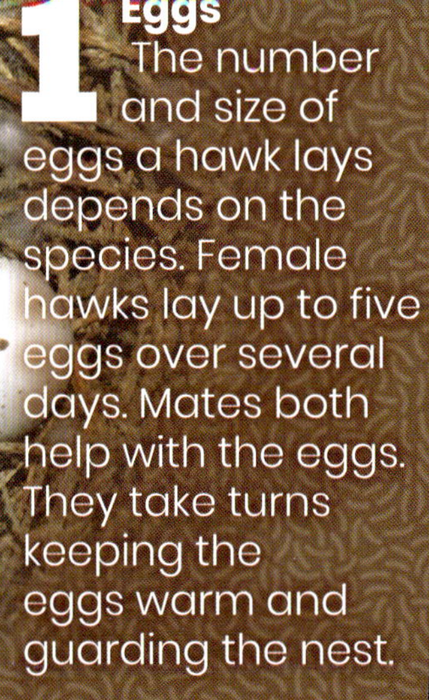

1 Eggs

The number and size of eggs a hawk lays depends on the species. Female hawks lay up to five eggs over several days. Mates both help with the eggs. They take turns keeping the eggs warm and guarding the nest.

2 Nestlings

Hawk eggs hatch several weeks after being laid. A baby hawk is called a nestling or an eyas. Nestlings are covered in fluffy feathers known as down. They are fed torn-up food. When young hawks are about four to seven weeks old, they begin to fly. Soon, they start to hunt on their own.

3 Adults

Some hawk species reuse the same nest every year. They use sticks, bark, and other materials to fix or add to it. In rare cases, hawks can live more than 20 years in nature. **Captive** birds sometimes live into their 30s.

What Do Hawks Eat?

All hawks eat meat. They typically hunt for food. However, they also eat dead animals that they find or steal from other **predators**. The type of food a hawk eats depends on its habitat and species. Some hawks are specialists, eating mostly one type of prey. Others eat many different foods. Hawks may eat other birds, along with mammals, reptiles, amphibians, fish, and insects.

Hawks hunt by swooping down on their prey. Then, they use their sharp talons to catch it. Hawks may eat small prey on the ground or carry it back to a perch first. They will often eat larger prey on the ground.

When carrying a fish it has caught, an osprey turns it so that the fish faces forward. This helps the bird carry it through the air more easily.

Some hawks are found in cities. These birds eat common urban animals, such as squirrels, rats, and mice.

Hawks around the World

Many different species of hawks **breed**, nest, and soar around the world. Each is adapted to survive in its home habitats.

RED-TAILED HAWK

Red-tailed hawks are known for their colorful tails. These birds live in many different habitats, including woodlands, deserts, and grasslands. What they eat depends on where they live. Their diet can include small mammals, lizards, fish, and other birds. Red-tailed hawks are common, numbering more than 2 million in the Americas and the Caribbean.

HARRIS'S HAWK

Harris's hawks live in woodlands and deserts in the Americas. Unlike most raptors, these hawks often live and hunt in groups. This helps them catch bigger prey. Groups can include up to seven birds, with one dominant female. This bird leads the group and lays the eggs. All birds in the group care for the nest. If it is threatened, one hawk will give an alarm call. Then, all the birds will attack the intruder.

OSPREY

Ospreys can be found either **wintering** or breeding on every continent except Antarctica. They can live almost anywhere near a body of water. Fish make up almost all of an osprey's food. An osprey flies above the water until it sees a fish below. Diving down, it hits the water feet first and grabs its food. Ospreys may go completely under the water when hunting.

NORTHERN GOSHAWK

Northern goshawks are large forest raptors. They can catch prey weighing up to half their weight. Goshawks are found in the mountains and forests of Europe, Asia, and North America. Mated pairs aggressively defend their nests from threats. Northern goshawks are quite vocal. Both males and females make wailing sounds when they enter or leave the nest.

Hawk Encounters

Hawks can be dangerous to people. They will defend their nest from threats such as wildlife, humans, or pets. Hawks will dive at threats that come too close to a nest. In some cases, government officials may have to relocate the nests of aggressive hawks. Some species, such as the ferruginous hawk, will abandon their nests if humans disturb them. Staying away from hawk nests helps keep both humans and hawks safe.

Binoculars or telescopes can be used to view hawks migrating or soaring overhead. People can watch hawk nests online using webcams. This allows people to view hatchlings and their parents up close without bothering them.

Ridgway's hawks often build nests on top of those of a smaller bird species, the palmchat. They do this without harming the birds nesting below.

Ospreys will build nests on any tall structures near water, including power line poles. This can lead to fires, so people and groups often build tall platforms near these structures to give ospreys safe places to nest.

Protecting Hawks

Hawks have very few predators. Their biggest threats come from people. Like many other raptors, hawks face impacts from habitat loss from logging or construction. They are also affected by climate change, hunting, poisoning, and nest disturbances.

Some countries have laws protecting hawks from hunting and trapping. Many have also banned DDT, a poison used to stop pests. When birds eat these pests, the poison causes the shells of their eggs to break before hatching. **Conservation** programs have helped to pass laws protecting hawk habitats around the world.

Ridgway's Hawk Case Study

The Ridgway's hawk is critically endangered. At one point, the last 300 birds were all living in one park in the Dominican Republic. The hawks were disappearing because of habitat loss and hunting. Nestlings were also killed by **parasitic** insects. Today, a conservation project is now helping the hawks survive. It moves young hawks to new habitats to help spread the species. Bird-safe pesticides are being used to kill the parasites. Today, four times the nestlings survive. There are still fewer than 500 of these hawks, but their numbers are growing.

The Hawaiian hawk is only found in the U.S. state of Hawaii. This limited habitat, and the species' small population, means it is considered to be near threatened.

Hawk Conservation Status

Least Concern		Short-Tailed Hawk (*Buteo brachyurus*)
Near Threatened		
Vulnerable		Rufous-Tailed Hawk (*Buteo ventralis*)
Endangered		Gundlach's Hawk (*Accipiter gundlachi*)
Critically Endangered		Ridgway's Hawk (*Buteo ridgwayi*)
Extinct		

Hawk Quiz

1 How far can Swainson's hawks migrate?

2 Which species of hawk is known to hunt in groups?

3 What do ospreys close when they dive under water?

4 How many eggs do female hawks lay at a time?

5 What is another name for nestling hawks?

6 What shape are the wings of a forest hawk?

7 Which species of hawk builds its nest on top of another bird's nest?

8 What are a group of hawks in the sky called?

Answers:
1. More than 6,000 miles (9,600 km) each way **2.** Harris's hawk **3.** Their third eyelid **4.** Up to five **5.** Eyas **6.** Short and round wings **7.** Ridgway's hawk **8.** A kettle

Key Words

adaptations: changes in animals that help them survive in their environment

breed: have young

captive: not living in a natural habitat

conservation: preserving or protecting something

habitat: places where animals or plants normally live in nature

migrate: travel a long distance when the seasons change

parasitic: living on and feeding on another living thing

predators: animals that hunt other animals for food

prey: animals that are hunted by other animals for food

species: a group of animals with the same characteristics; members of a species can usually only breed with other members of that species

talons: sharp claws found on certain birds of prey

tropical: a warm area near the equator

wintering: spending the winter months in a location

Index

Get the best of both worlds.

AV2 bridges the gap between print and digital.

The expandable resources toolbar enables quick access to content including **videos**, **audio**, **activities**, **weblinks**, **slideshows**, **quizzes**, and **key words**.

Animated videos make static images come alive.

Resource icons on each page help readers to further **explore key concepts**.

Published by Lightbox Learning Inc.
276 5th Avenue, Suite 704 #917
New York, NY 10001
Website: www.openlightbox.com

Library of Congress Control Number: 2022938853

ISBN 978-1-7911-4706-8 (hardcover)
ISBN 978-1-7911-4707-5 (softcover)
ISBN 978-1-7911-4708-2 (multi-user eBook)

Printed in Guangzhou, China
1 2 3 4 5 6 7 8 9 0 26 25 24 23 22

072022
101121

Project Coordinator: John Willis
Designer: Terry Paulhus

Photo Credits
Every reasonable effort has been made to trace ownership and to obtain permission to reprint copyright material. The publisher would be pleased to have any errors or omissions brought to its attention so that they may be corrected in subsequent printings.
The publisher acknowledges Alamy, Minden Pictures, Getty Images, Shutterstock, and Wikimedia as its primary image suppliers for this title.